Original title:
The Mango's Melody

Copyright © 2025 Creative Arts Management OÜ
All rights reserved.

Author: Rosalie Bradford
ISBN HARDBACK: 978-1-80586-417-2
ISBN PAPERBACK: 978-1-80586-889-7

Sway of the Branches

Under the sun, a dance begins,
Branches bending, swaying grins,
A fruit so bright, with laughter shared,
Making monkeys joyfully ensnared.

Wind whistles through the leafy spree,
As squirrels join in, so wild and free.
The air is filled with fruity cheer,
While ants march on, their song sincere.

Tropic Tunes

Drums of nature play a tune,
Echoing 'neath the silver moon.
With each pluck, a giggle flows,
As every fruit in rhythm grows.

Laughter rings from trees so tall,
While toucans join the lively call.
The ground shakes with a joyful beat,
As nature's band accepts the heat.

Radiant Reflections

Sunshine sparkles on a stream,
Where fruits and fables weave a dream.
Chasing shadows, friends they play,
Bouncing colors brighten the day.

With every bite, a joke bestowed,
As laughter flows in fruity mode.
In this bright, amusing scene,
Life is juicy, sweet, and keen.

Harvested Chords

Gather 'round for the feast we made,
The fruits of laughter will not fade.
With every nibble, cheers erupt,
As everyone's in giggles, swooped!

   Plucking goodies from up high,
   Singing songs beneath the sky.
   Chords of taste and fun collide,
   As every joke takes us for a ride.

Sun-Kissed Notes

In the orchard where fruit swings,
Laughter dances, oh how it sings!
Juicy wonders hide on the floor,
While bees play tunes, forevermore.

Squirrels swing with acorn hats,
Shaking branches, wearing spats.
Nature's jesters, with tiny giggles,
Challenge each other with fruity wiggles.

Vibrant Rhythms

Beneath the sun, the fruits collide,
A bumpy ride, it's quite a slide!
Chasing shadows, rolling free,
With pips and peels, how funny they be!

A parrot squawks, a clever prank,
Stealing snacks from a fruit-filled tank.
Wait, what's that? A splash! Oh dear!
A fruit-fueled pie fight, let's all cheer!

Golden Harmonies

In a grove where giggles grow,
Melodies of mangoes steal the show.
The sunbeam dances on each cheek,
As playful antics reach their peak.

With every pluck, a silly joke,
The fruits burst out with laughter's poke.
Their sweet-filled laughter fills the air,
Chasing the clouds, without a care.

Echoes of Sweetness

Beneath the trees, a chorus plays,
Mushy mishaps fill the days.
Fragrant tunes of ripe delight,
Tickle toes, oh what a sight!

Spinning fruits in a fruity dance,
Take a slip — oh, what a chance!
Splashes, smirks, and fruit confetti,
Life is sweet, and oh so petty!

Honeyed Drop of Sunshine

In the garden, fruits are bold,
One drop of sweetness, stories told.
Bouncing bugs, a dance they weave,
Underneath the shade, we believe.

Lemon leaps, and cherries cheer,
With every bite, the giggles near.
Nature's jokes in every bite,
Oh, what a funny fruit delight!

A Chorus of Ripeness

In the market, colors collide,
Peaches play and lemons slide.
Bananas toss their golden hats,
While berries sing with silly chats.

Ripe tomatoes wear a grin,
A veggie party, let's begin!
Cucumber hats and carrot ties,
Laughter grows beneath the skies.

Whispers of Lush Canopies

Under leaves, a secret spreads,
Coconut laughs, while watermelon treads.
Mangoes swing from breezy boughs,
Pineapple chuckles with furry cows.

A jester's fruit, oh what a sight,
Nature's comedy, pure delight.
Swinging branches, silly sounds,
Giggles rooted in the grounds.

Sweetness Under the Golden Skies

Sunny days bring forth the grin,
With every fruit, a tiny spin.
Oranges juggling down the lane,
Causing bursts of fruity rain.

Sugar ants perform their dance,
While apples roll in goofy prance.
Under skies, a cheerful spree,
Laughing fruits, come join the glee!

Orchard's Overtones

In the orchard, fruit does sway,
Bouncing to the breeze's play.
Dropping laughs from branches high,
Tasty bits that make us sigh.

Squirrels giggle, chasing tails,
Catching fruit as it trails.
Birds dance with their silly songs,
Nature hums where fun belongs.

Harmonizing With Nature

Dancing leaves, a jitterbug,
The grass gives a playful shrug.
Frogs croak beats, out of tune,
Playing under the bright moon.

Bees buzzing like a band,
Crafting music through the land.
Ticklish winds, they twist and twirl,
Nature's giggles start to whirl.

Luscious Musings

Juicy spheres on branches bold,
Laughing whispers, tales are told.
One fell, landed with a bounce,
"Catch me if you can!" it trounced.

Friends unite for tasty fun,
Chomping 'til the day is done.
Many flavors, smiles all around,
In this laughter, joy is found.

Rhythm of Ripeness

Plump and shining, fruits on show,
Wobbling with a cheeky flow.
Dance off shelves, don't miss your chance,
Who knew fruits could really prance?

With a jig, they roll and spin,
A bouncy game, let's begin!
In this orchard, fun's the theme,
Fruity laughter's quite the dream.

Nature's Song

In the garden, birds do sing,
A parrot jives and starts to swing.
The flowers giggle in delight,
As ants do march, quite out of sight.

A butterfly with fancy flair,
Flits and floats without a care.
Bees buzz tunes of sweet surprise,
While frogs do croak their lullabies.

Tropical Crescendo

A coconut rolls down the street,
While monkeys dance on nimble feet.
The breeze, it teases, sways the palm,
And every leaf begs for a jam.

A pineapple wears a funky hat,
While lizards strut, oh how they chat!
The sun beats down, it's quite the scene,
As laughter flows where fun's routine.

Lush Landscapes in Verse

In verdant fields where laughter rings,
Peacocks flaunt their feathered blings.
The daisies play a game of peek,
With squirrels chasing, oh so sleek.

Rain drops tap on leafy drums,
While a sleepy sloth hums and hums.
A turtle moves with all its might,
Yet dreams of racing through the night.

Colorful Chords

A chubby frog sings off-key,
While crickets join in harmony.
The vibrant hues of daydsky glow,
As rainbows dance, put on a show.

A goldfish leaps from bowl to sky,
While clouds float by, they just can't fly.
The world's a stage of joyful quirks,
In every nook, where laughter lurks.

Breezes of Bliss

In the orchard, fruits do sway,
With clueless bees, they dance and play.
A squirrel slips, lands in a bush,
While giggling fowl create a hush.

Bright sunbeams tickle leaves all day,
A pig spins round, now what a display!
Laughter echoes through the sweet air,
As laughter and joy dance everywhere.

Sunlit Cadence

Bouncing balls of yellow light,
Chasing shadows, oh, what a sight!
A monkey swings from branch to tree,
Grabs his tail, then shouts with glee.

Friends gather 'round with joyous cheer,
Tales of mishaps, "Oh dear, oh dear!"
Slipping on peels, down they go,
Like silly dancers, a comical show.

Fragrant Rhapsody

Scented breezes fill the air,
With giggles high and carefree flair.
A cat upon a fence, quite stout,
Eats a slice — it quickly pouts.

With fruity treats and jolly fun,
They splash around 'til day is done.
Whispers of sweetness, jokes abound,
In this fruity place, laughter is found.

Verse of the Tree

Underneath the leafy shade,
A monkey's pranks begin to invade.
Banana peels fly left and right,
They're managing quite the silly sight.

A turtle sneezes, sends a shout,
The whole gang laughs, there's no doubt.
As shadows grow and sunbeams flee,
They find their joy, beneath the tree.

Song of Juicy Reverie

Oh, the fruit that swings from the trees,
Plump and fuzzy, oh what a tease!
With a giggle, it drops to the ground,
A juicy splat, what a silly sound!

Bumbling bees dance in the air,
Wobbling ants join, without a care.
Underneath the sun, they prance and sway,
To a rhythm of sweetness, here to stay!

Lush Dreams Beneath the Sun

In the shade of leaves, we find our fun,
Laughter echoes where the days are spun.
A fruit feud brews, oh what a sight,
Hilarity reigns with every bite!

Sipping nectar, bees wear tiny hats,
And squirrels plot while avoiding spats.
Each juicy morsel, a burst of cheer,
Come join the feast, the fun is near!

A Dance of Harvest and Delight

In the orchard, a party begins,
With fruit so ripe, nobody sins.
Peeling laughter like a skin so thin,
Only the brave dare to dig in!

Birds in bow ties gather above,
Chirping tunes of fruit-filled love.
As they drop, the fruits giggle and roll,
In this juicy jamboree, we all stroll!

Aroma of Sun-Kissed Bliss

Wafting scents of joy take flight,
In the orchard's heart, such pure delight.
Fruits glisten like tiny suns,
Every bite, laughter runs!

Dancing squirrels try to impress,
While chatting birds seek no less.
With every peel, the day's a show,
What is this magic? Oh, let it flow!

Lyrical Harvest

In a grove where fruit takes flight,
A quirky dance, oh what a sight!
The trees all sway, they laugh and play,
While juicy jokes peel night away.

Beneath the sun, a fruit parade,
With every bounce, a burst displayed.
The laughter ripens, sweet and bold,
As stories in the juice unfold.

Serenade of the Tropics

A yellow glob, so round and bright,
Winks at me from morning light.
I reached for one, it slipped away,
And rolled down to the bay to play.

The crabs all dance, the gulls hum tunes,
While under shade, the fun fest looms.
It juggles laughs, this slippery fruit,
As tangoed ants join in pursuit.

Sunkissed Sonnet

With sunshine painted on its skin,
It twirls about, with joyful grin.
A fruity laugh, a light-hearted bounce,
In every slice, a giggle pounce.

Each bite a treasure, sweet delight,
It tickles tongues, ignites the night.
With every drop of sticky cheer,
The world grows bright, the worries clear.

Synthesis of Flavors

A fruity mix, oh what a blend,
It tricks the tongue, a juicy friend.
With every zing, a chuckle's born,
It struts around like it's adorned.

In kitchens bright, it plays a part,
With sprinkles of fun, it steals the heart.
From smoothies wild to pies that sing,
This fruit of joy—what joy it brings!

Lush Lyricism in Every Slice

In the garden where laughter grows,
Juicy jewels hang in rows.
Each slice a giggle, sweet and bright,
Bursting with flavor, pure delight.

Rolling in sunshine, giggles abound,
Chasing the shadows on the ground.
With every bite, a smile takes flight,
Your taste buds dance, oh what a sight!

Spilling juice like silly jokes,
Tickling tongues, we're happy folks.
Wacky flavors dare to tease,
Nature's comedy with such ease.

So slice that fruit, don't hesitate,
Join the fun, celebrate!
Lush lyrics in each sweet bite,
A laughter-filled, fruity delight!

Feel the Sun's Embrace on Juicy Dreams

Sunshine dances on fruity peaks,
Where sweetness whispers, giggling speaks.
Each drop of juice, a goofy cheer,
Sips of joy, bring friends so near.

With every bite, a chuckle blooms,
Flavorful jokes fill all the rooms.
Squirting laughter, bright and bold,
Fruity tales, a joy to behold.

We juggle slices, what a sight!
Falling fruit in sheer delight.
Sun-kissed sweetness, grin and beam,
Chase your dreams, live the dream team!

So slice away, let laughter soar,
With juicy wonders, we want more!
A sunny embrace in every taste,
Life's too short for any waste!

Nature's Opus in the Orchard

In an orchard where silliness reigns,
Fruits compose the wackiest chains.
Each pluck a note in nature's song,
Harmonies where we all belong.

The trees sway, conduct with flair,
Ticklish breezes tease our hair.
Fruity puns shake the sturdy boughs,
Laughter echoes, take a bow!

Sliced symphonies on our plates,
Crunchy giggles, no debates.
Juicy rhythms, a playful tease,
Nature's humor, sure to please.

So grab a fruit and make a tune,
Dance with sunshine, hum with the moon.
In the orchard, joy takes flight,
Nature's opus, pure delight!

Fruitsong of the Sun-Drenched Grove

In the grove where sunlight beams,
Fragrant whispers spark our dreams.
Laughter ripens on the vine,
Singing songs, oh how divine!

Each fruit a note in a fruity scale,
Tickling our senses, never stale.
Bouncing berries, dancing peaches,
Joyous laughter, love it teaches.

Chomp and giggle, what a treat,
Juicy madness, can't be beat.
A chorus of flavors, oh what fun,
Grove of voices, never done!

So join the feast, let's sing along,
With every bite, we're feeling strong.
In this sun-kissed, silly grove,
Fruitsong plays, laughter rove!

Dance of Flavor and Fragrance

In the orchard, fruits do sway,
Bouncing like kids in a play.
Sticky fingers, laughter's sound,
Sweetness in the air abound.

Chasing bees, they hum a tune,
Dressed in sun, like a cartoon.
Lizards join with a little jig,
While squirrels dance, so big and sprig.

A fruit or two, they lift and toss,
Apples pout, but mangos gloss.
In this fest, no time for sleep,
Nature's rhythm, oh so deep.

Giggling fruits on branches swing,
To the uproar of birds that sing.
Whimsical whispers in the breeze,
A fruity party, if you please!

Melodies from the Orchard's Embrace

In the orchard, where dreams play,
Ripened laughter grows each day.
Fruits wear hats made of the sun,
Joking 'round, it's so much fun.

Bananas swing, the lemons cheer,
Pineapples wiggle, without fear.
With each plop, they drop and roll,
Nature hoots, it's quite the stroll.

Dance in circles, round and round,
As shadows stretch upon the ground.
Even the roots join in, you see,
Funky vibes from the bottom tree.

Scented breezes play their part,
With sweet rhythms, they warm the heart.
Every flutter, every laugh,
Turns this orchard to a craft!

Sunlit Riffs of Nature's Bounty

Sunny days and smiles galore,
Fruits burst forth, who could ask for more?
Jive and wiggle, grape and pear,
Sipping nectar, happiness in the air.

Blueberries boast with sassy flair,
They bubble up, toss back their hair.
Peaches blush and giggle loud,
In this orchard, all are proud.

Limes groove to a citrus beat,
While strawberries tap their petite feet.
A juicy jam session begins,
Where every fruit is here to win!

Under sun, the harvest plays,
Each sweet note a fruity phrase.
Laughter echoes, oh what fun,
In this garden, everyone's won!

Harmonies of Petals and Pulp

Petals twirl in a fruity dance,
All around, there's a sweet romance.
Grapefruits giggle, oranges glide,
While daisies join the joyride.

Figs flirt with the morning breeze,
Lemons laugh as they tease the trees.
In this parade, all's in tune,
Life's a melody, under the moon.

Choruses formed by bees and bugs,
On the leaves, they give warm hugs.
Every bloom has its part to play,
In this orchestra of a sunlit day.

With each burst of vibrant hue,
The fruits burst forth with a funny view.
Nature's symphony, oh so bright,
Together, we dance into the night!

Ripe Echoes

In the tree, oh what a sight,
Mangoes hanging, oh so bright.
A monkey swings with glee to see,
His fruity feast, a jubilee.

Juicy splats upon the ground,
A squishy dance, oh such a sound.
Bumblebees march, in a line,
Buzzing tunes, quite the design.

Children laugh, they skip about,
Under the shade, they twist and shout.
With sticky hands and grins so wide,
Tropical smiles, they cannot hide.

In each bite, a giggle found,
One slips, falls, and rolls around.
Gone with the thrill, up in the air,
The mango lands—another dare!

Melody beneath the Leaves

A fruit gathers, pink and gold,
Whispers shared, stories told.
Silly squirrels join the fun,
Taking bets on which will run.

Underneath the leafy shade,
A dance of shadows, mischief made.
Branches sway, a wobbly tune,
Plucking fruit like a cartoon.

Slips and trips, the laughter grows,
Friendship's blend in juice that flows.
A splash of fun, with giggly bites,
Echoes of joy on sunny nights.

They juggle mangoes, not for a feat,
One rolls away, kissing their feet.
The chase is on, the crowd's delight,
Chasing fruit 'til the end of light.

Lush Resonance

A fruit dropped down with a thud,
A royal splat, oh what a flood!
From the tree, it ends its flight,
Bouncing round like sheer delight.

Silly parakeets, what a show,
Join in antics, to and fro.
One has a mango, what a steal,
Goes for a ride, oh what a deal!

Laughter swirls with fruity scents,
In this world, there's no pretense.
Sticky faces, wild with cheer,
They share bites, dispelling fear.

Ecstatic giggles run amok,
Underneath the tree, they flock.
As mangoes fall and spirits high,
The day rolls on, and so do I!

Ripened Whispers of Summer

In the tree, I spy a prize,
A round delight, much to my surprise.
With a wink and a sway, it calls my name,
I'll climb this trunk, it's all a game!

Sticky hands and juice that drips,
I'm dodging ants and sweetened slips.
Each bite a giggle, each taste a cheer,
Who knew summer could bring such sheer?

A toss to friends, it flies like a pro,
We laugh and grin as they lay low.
A fruity feast where fun's the plan,
In this orchard, we're the fruit-loving clan!

So let us dance in this golden light,
With every slip, we giggle in flight.
A summer's tale of sweet delight,
In laughter and fruit, everything feels right!

Sweet Serenade of the Orchard

A song from branches up high does play,
In whispers of green on a sunny day.
The fruit winks bright, a cheeky tease,
Come taste my sweetness, if you please!

With each bouncy step, the fun begins,
I stumble upon a treasure of skins.
A slippery slip turns into a glide,
In this orchard, we take it in stride!

The juice cascades, a sugary flow,
I laugh as it lands on my toe.
A day of glee with sticky care,
In this fruity game, we all must share!

We gather round with laughter and cheer,
As sweet melodies are all we hear.
In each juicy bite, we find our song,
With smiles so bright, we can't go wrong!

Golden Hues in a Sunlit Breeze

In a patch of sun where the golden glow beams,
Laughter spills over like flowing streams.
With a swing and a hop, we reach for the prize,
A burst of sunshine right before our eyes!

Oh, the joy of a plunge into fruity bliss,
A squishy delight you just can't miss!
Tommy slips and Gary grins,
While juices trickle and mischief begins.

Friends hold their bellies, giggling so loud,
Chasing each other, feeling so proud.
A fruit fight starts, what a crazy sight,
Are we farmers or jesters? Oh, what a delight!

So we savor the day when it's sunny and clear,
With a zest for fun and a cold glass of cheer.
Each bite, a party, a dance in disguise,
In this golden glow, our spirits all rise!

Tropical Harmonies in Each Bite

In the warm embrace of a tropical breeze,
We gather around like buzzing bees.
With laughter as bright as the sun in the sky,
We slice up the joy and let out a sigh!

Oh, the flavor that tickles and dances so fine,
It's a melody sweet from the vine.
Spinning and twirling with fruity delight,
We craft our own tunes on this sunlit night!

I slip on some juice, then pop up with flair,
A splash of laughter, a sticky affair.
We toss fruit high, it's a comedy act,
With each bursting giggle, there's nothing we lack.

So let us all gather, it's a flavor parade,
With friends by our side, no need for charade.
In every sweet bite, we find our own rhyme,
In this playful orchard, we dance through time!

Ripe Reverie

In the tree, a treasure swings,
A fruit that laughs, and joy it brings.
When it drops, a thud so loud,
The startled birds fly from the crowd.

Sticky fingers, faces bright,
Beneath the sun, pure delight.
We giggle as we stain our clothes,
With every slice, hilarity grows.

Sipping juice, it drips and splats,
We squeal like happy, chubby cats.
Oh, the pits, they fly like darts,
Launch them high, it's art in parts!

A ripe reverie in the air,
Laughter fills, floats everywhere.
With every bite, a joyful cheer,
We dance, we laugh, with glee sincere.

Songs of the Orchard

In the orchard, notes take flight,
Fruits are dancing left and right.
Melodies of laughter soar,
As juice cascades upon the floor.

Baboons sing, with voices loud,
The squirrels join, a happy crowd.
Wobbling rabbits in a line,
Bouncing to the rhythm, feeling fine.

Verses drip from every leaf,
A symphony, beyond belief.
With each bite, a chorus bursts,
Sweet and tangy, it quenches thirsts.

Oh, the songs that trees can share,
With nature's band, we have no care.
Under the sky, in fruity bliss,
Every note, a juicy kiss.

Juicy Lyrics

Sticky fingers, fruity beats,
Laughter simmers in the streets.
Slicing wedges, summer's cheer,
Juicy tales for all to hear.

Giggles rise with every squirt,
Pips fly out, a fruity spurt.
We brave the mess, no fear in sight,
Creating art in every bite.

Fruits wear hats made of green leaves,
Chasing friends like busy bees.
"Catch that pit!" we shout with glee,
A party hosted by the tree.

Juicy lyrics fill the air,
With every laugh, we shed our care.
Moments sweet, as sunbeams glow,
In every drip, our joy will flow.

Glistening Harmonies

Golden globes that shine so bright,
Glistening treasures in the light.
Swaying gently with the breeze,
Laughter mingles with the leaves.

Sliding down the rinds we go,
Pits like marbles, round and slow.
We slip and slide in pure delight,
Giggling echoes day and night.

Harmonies of taste take flight,
Dancing flavors, pure delight.
As juice runs down our chins,
We find the fun that always wins.

Underneath the branches' sway,
In glistening hues, we play all day.
With every bite, our hearts take wing,
To the playful songs that summer brings.

Fruity Harmonies

In a garden bright and bold,
Fruits gather, stories told.
Bananas dance with juicy pride,
While cherries giggle, side by side.

Lemons strum, making sour tunes,
As pears hum soft, beneath the moons.
Grapes wear hats, quite out of style,
Making everyone laugh a while.

Each fruit a note in playful cheer,
Combining smiles, spreading beer.
With every bite, a sound so sweet,
A fruity chorus, can't be beat!

Melons roll and plums pirouette,
Creating laughs we'll never forget.
In this orchard, joy's in store,
Fruity harmonies forevermore!

Tones of Tranquility

Peaches whisper in the breeze,
While apricots float like honey bees.
A quiet giggle ripples through,
As berries wear their morning dew.

Watermelons laugh with every slice,
Their juicy interiors, oh so nice.
Kiwis chuckle, green and round,
In this paradise, joy is found.

Each fruit has secrets, stories to share,
With smooth melodies that fill the air.
Graceful laughter, soft and bright,
In fruity tones, pure delight!

Limes roll over, causing a scene,
Their zesty joy, so evergreen.
In orchards lush, serenity flows,
The sweetest tunes, everybody knows!

Enchanted Orchards

In orchards where the sunlight beams,
Fruits plot mischief, share their dreams.
Apples chase away the gloom,
While figs play hide-and-seek in bloom.

Grapes dress up, a fancy spree,
As oranges sing in harmony.
Beneath the shade, they spin and twirl,
An enchanted world begins to swirl.

Passion fruits with silly grins,
Tell how laughter truly begins.
Starfruit winks, a cosmic cheer,
Inviting all to dance and leer!

So join the fun, there's space for all,
In this jovial, fruity ball.
Where laughter ripens on every tree,
Enchanted orchards, wild and free!

Sweet Summer Echoes

In summer's glow, the fruits all sing,
Echoing joy in a balmy fling.
Lemons jive, and limes do sway,
As berries laugh throughout the day.

With every bite, a giggle bursts,
A juicy fun; it quells all thirsts.
Peaches blush with a cheeky grin,
In this dance, let the fun begin!

Pineapples wear their crowns so grand,
As watermelons form a band.
Together they create sweet sounds,
In summer echoes, joy abounds!

Fruity antics, bright and merry,
Bring smiles like a candy cherry.
So come and taste this sunny cheer,
In sweet summer, laughter's near!

Sweetness in the Air

In a tree so tall and wide,
Lemons thought they had the pride.
But then came a fruit, orange and round,
With laughter that burst, oh so profound.

Squirrels danced with nutty flair,
While birds chirped tunes beyond compare.
All around, a zesty cheer,
As fruity pranksters gathered near.

A picnic spread with giggles gleamed,
Grapes rolled in, the table seemed.
Bananas slipped and took a dive,
In this fruit fiesta, all felt alive!

Oh, to be a fruit in this scene,
With silly antics, never mean.
The air was sweet, the jokes flew high,
In nature's party, oh my, oh my!

Melody of the Tropics

Under sun-kissed skies so bright,
The coconuts joined in the fight.
Bouncing on waves, they had their say,
While pineapples sang and swayed away.

Mangoes giggled, rolled on grass,
A silly game, oh what a class!
They tossed each other, plump and round,
As laughter echoed all around.

Papayas joined with a jazzy beat,
While limes danced with wobbly feet.
The rhythm surged, everyone swayed,
In this fruity band, no one was afraid.

Beneath the shade, a breeze would stir,
As grapes spun tales with a little slur.
Tropical tunes, such playful cheer,
In this fruity world, all had no fear!

Rhythms of Delight

In a garden bright with giggles loud,
Each fruit took turns, oh so proud.
Bananas slipped on their own peel,
Creating chaos, what a big deal!

Berries burst with laughter sweet,
While guavas wobbled on their feet.
The rhythm bustled, everyone joined,
As fruity pranks completely coined.

Kiwi tried a dance, not so neat,
With every twirl, fell on its feet.
Oranges rolled and cheered so loud,
As laughter formed a wacky crowd.

Underneath the sun's warm glow,
Fruits made trouble, putting on a show.
With every laugh and every cheer,
The rhythms of delight rang loud and clear!

Dancing Shadows

As night fell slow, the fruits found glee,
Dancing shadows beneath the tree.
Mangoes jived with cheeky flair,
Casting silhouettes that filled the air.

Coconuts wobbled, attempting a sway,
While bananas joined in, come what may.
The moonlight chuckled at their moves,
As they grooved along, in silly grooves.

Limes spun around, a dizzy display,
Fruits laughing hard as they lost their way.
Twirling against the starry sky,
Each shadow a tale, oh how they fly!

With every step, a new joke brewed,
In this moonlit dance, they all were glued.
As shadows laughed and shadows played,
In fruity fun, all sorrows swayed!

The Flavorful Ballad of Youth

In a garden where laughter grows,
Tiny hands pick fruits in rows.
Juices drip down chubby chins,
Fruity faces with cheeky grins.

Underneath the sun's embrace,
We dance with joy, a lively race.
Sporting pits like crowns we wear,
The sweetest taste, beyond compare.

Mom shouts, 'Don't waste that delight!'
But who can resist the fruity fight?
With every squirt and sticky mess,
Our giggles grow, oh what a bless!

As shadows stretch and laughter fades,
We're kings and queens in fruit arcades.
Today, we're young and never done,
In this ballad, we're all but one.

Sunkissed Lullabies on My Tongue

A sunbeam kisses every bite,
Bursting flavors, pure delight.
Sunkissed sticky, oh so nice,
I could rave about this twice!

The sign reads, 'Not for the shy!'
But daring kids just swoop and fly.
Caution tossed like peels around,
In sweet harmony, we are bound.

Tasting sunshine on my lip,
A flavor-fueled, joyous trip.
With laughter loud, we sing in sync,
Between the bites, we barely think!

In this playground of surprise,
Fruity pigments fill the skies.
Every laugh a note we strum,
In echo chambers, 'Taste the fun!'

Serenading the Summer's Abundance

Sweetness reigns in summer's air,
With every fruit a tale to share.
We sing and twirl beneath the sun,
Where juicy rivers make us run.

The trees sway, a graceful dance,
And plop, a fruit—what a chance!
Hilarity bursts with each big bite,
A flavor fight, oh what a sight!

Under shades of emerald green,
We munch on treasures, pure and clean.
Spilling juice while taking aim,
A sticky war, oh what a game!

With giggles floating on the breeze,
The bees join in, they know our keys.
In these moments, wild and fun,
Our laughter weaves 'til day is done.

Chants of the Tropical Trees

Oh, hear the whispers from the grove,
Where sticky treasure tales are trove.
Pits and peels, the war declared,
On nature's feast, all are prepared.

Ripe and round, they tumble down,
A merry group with sullen frown.
But once that flavor hits the spot,
Our worries fade—what a plot!

In bunches, friends come, just to share,
An invitation to the fair.
Laughter rings where sweetness flows,
As fruit confetti from the rows.

We chant the tunes of summer's trees,
In joyful chaos, feel the breeze.
With every bite, a note we sing,
In nature's choir, we're the kings!

Nature's Crescendo

In the orchard, fruits do sway,
With a dance that steals the day.
Bumblebees hum along the tune,
While squirrels wear hats made of moon.

A parrot sings a silly song,
While frogs jump in, they all get along.
The thumping base of the old tree trunk,
Makes even the grumpiest monkey skunk.

Each leaf joins in the merry cheer,
Tickling the breeze like a ticklish deer.
Laughter echoes from every bough,
As nature plays its jokes right now.

In this patch of vibrant green,
We dance like no one ever seen.
So come join in this silly show,
Where even the flowers put on a glow.

Sunkissed Embrace

Golden rays bounce off the skin,
Sunshine glows, let the fun begin.
A lizard basks in this sunlit glee,
While ants march on in rhythmic spree.

The breeze flirts with ladybugs bright,
Twisting and twirling in sheer delight.
A butterfly trips, laughing with grace,
As flowers giggle in colorful lace.

"Oh look!" chirps a bird with flair,
"Who wore it best? That bee over there!"
Nature's runway, a glitzy parade,
Where laughter blossoms without a charade.

As the sky turns a rosy hue,
We gather close, just me and you.
In this sunny embrace, let's chill,
With silly smiles, our hearts will thrill.

Juicy Notes in the Breeze

Juicy fruits hang low and round,
While giggles fill the air with sound.
Caterpillars don their best attire,
Wiggling to tunes, never tire.

A fruit fly comments, "Do I look fab?"
As worms clamor for the latest jab.
Crisp bites echo from every branch,
As critters join in a quirky dance.

A robin tries to hit a high note,
While a wise owl giggles and gloats.
"I prefer jazz, my little friends,"
Says the tree trunk as the fun never ends.

Cherries blush with a vibrant grin,
As laughter rolls on the merry wind.
In this fruity fest, all gets bright,
Where nature's giggles bring pure delight.

Whispering Leaves

Leaves chatter softly in the breeze,
Sharing secrets like old tease.
A mischievous vine hides with glee,
Playing tricks on the curious bee.

"Did you hear what the grass said?!
My blades are sharper than your head!"
Roots chuckle beneath the ground,
While flowers prance in colorful round.

A squirrel drops acorns with flair,
As branches chuckle, light as air.
In this park, carefree and spry,
Even the clouds roll by with a sigh.

So let's join in this funny tale,
Where joys of nature set the scale.
With every rustle, laugh, and tease,
We find pure fun in whispering leaves.

Fruitful Whispers

A fruit in my hand, it winks with zest,
Its skin so bright, it's surely dressed.
I take a bite, oh what a splash,
Juicy sweetness makes me laugh in a flash.

The neighbors stare, they shake their heads,
How can one fruit bring such spreads?
In fruity fights, we toss and play,
Catching laughter, come what may!

With sticky hands and giggles round,
We're the silliest fruit lovers found.
A twist, a turn, a slippery slide,
We roll and tumble, joy cannot hide.

In the fruit bowl's heart, we hold our throne,
A jester's crown, in fruity tone.
Whispers of fun, we dance and sway,
In this tasty game, let's shout hooray!

Symphony of the Orchard

In an orchard bright, a band did play,
With fruits as instruments, hip-hip-hooray!
An apple on drums, with a pear on the flute,
Bananas on maracas, what a silly hoot!

The berries burst in a jazzy swing,
While citrus joins in, making hearts sing.
A watermelon choir belts out with glee,
"Let's dance and be fruity, you and me!"

The wind joins the tune, a breeze so spry,
Tickles the leaves as they flutter and fly.
In this zesty concert, laughter combines,
Creating a wonder, sweet grapevines and pines.

As laughter erupts, the show comes alive,
Each fruit with a joke, and smiles we derive.
In this vibrant orchard, a joyful spree,
With funny tunes echoing wild and free!

Juicy Serenade

In a garden fair, where fruits take lead,
A serenade of laughter is all we need.
Mangoes sway, with cheeky grins,
While cherries tease, in playful spins.

A cantaloupe croons a tune so sweet,
"Come dance with me, let's skip a beat!"
Peaches skitter, jiggling around,
As giggles and chuckles are heard abound.

From every branch, a jolly retreat,
Fruit do the cha-cha, oh what a feat!
With puddles of juice, we slip and slide,
In this juicy fiesta, let joy be our guide.

Beneath the sun's gaze, with laughter in tow,
We frolic in fun, let good feelings grow.
In every sweet bite, a surprise awaits,
As nature's orchestra laughs, and celebrates!

Harmonies of Honeyed Sun

Under honeyed rays, where sweet breezes blow,
Soft laughter ignites in the sunlight's glow.
With fruits bouncing high, in an airy embrace,
We giggle and roll, a delightful race.

A kiwi on skates, oh what a sight!
Sliding and spinning, with pure delight.
Grapes form a line, doing their dance,
One silly slip leads to laughter's enhance.

Bananas on bicycles zooming with glee,
Each twist and turn, adds more to the spree.
Fruits in a frenzy, all colors unite,
Creating a circus, a whimsical flight.

As daylight fades, the music won't stop,
With fruity bravado, we joyfully hop.
In this sun-kissed haven of fun and cheer,
We toast to the laughter, together we steer!

Melodies of Maturity

In the orchard, laughter grows,
Fruits dance in silly rows,
Ripening with cheeky glee,
Juicy jokes from tree to tree.

Oh the weight of life we bear,
Peeling skin, we strip with care,
Sweet and sour, life's the blend,
Punchlines ripen 'round the bend.

Late-night chats with plump old pears,
Tell tales of their peeling cares,
Life's a jest till you look ripe,
Find the fun in every type.

So let's laugh with fruit so wise,
Underneath those sunny skies,
Laughter shared among the trees,
Maturity with a side of freeze.

Whimsical Fruitscape

In a garden full of cheer,
Bouncy berries rolling near,
Grapes giggle, apples grin,
Nature's play begins again.

Citrus laugh with zesty zest,
Bananas chatting, looking best,
Peaches puffed and prickly pears,
Ready for their fruit-filled flares!

Occasionally a fruit will trip,
Splattering juice, a funny slip,
Twisting vines that play this game,
Fruitful antics, never tame.

In this world of fruity flair,
Whimsical fun, beyond compare,
With each bite and each grin wide,
Joyous vibes can't be denied!

Sweet Sunshine Symphony

The sun shines down, a golden tune,
Melodious moments, afternoons,
With fruits that swing and sway with grace,
Sweet delights in every place.

Watermelon serenade starts,
Strumming hearts and juicy parts,
Mangoes join in with a swing,
Together, making sweet hearts sing.

Lemon rinds, the witty jest,
Citrus zingers, we're impressed,
Harmony in flavors bright,
Symphony bursts in pure delight.

So take a bite, let laughter soar,
Join the chorus, want some more?
With every taste, the fun will bloom,
A simply sweet and sunny room.

Swaying with the Seasons

As summer waves, the dancers spin,
Fruits parade, they laugh and grin,
Cherries twirl, with shimmery flair,
Swirling joy fills the warm air.

Autumn's chill cannot deter,
Pears and figs stir up a stir,
Falling leaves, a playful race,
Fruity giggles fill the space.

In winter's chill, we snuggle tight,
Zesty citrus brings delight,
Snap your fingers, clap your hands,
Even cold can't cool our plans.

Spring arrives with fresh new tunes,
Budding fruits, the bright festoons,
With each season, laughter grows,
Swaying sweetly, nature knows!

The Dance of Sunshine and Sweetness

In a grove where laughter grows,
Fruit flirts with the breezy blows,
Pigeons prance on branches high,
As giggles rain from the blue sky.

Wiggly worms on an old tree swing,
Spinning tales of summer fling,
Ants bopping in their tiny shoes,
With juicy fruits to share their blues.

Lemons leap, and oranges spin,
During sunset's golden grin,
Bananas make a jazzy beat,
As coconuts tap their little feet.

Laughter echoes through the night,
Chasing shadows, what a sight!
Under a moon, the fun won't stop,
As fruits and critters dance and hop.

Singing Under a Tropical Canopy

Beneath the leaves, the critters sing,
Of berries bright and sweet spring fling,
Lizards laugh with a jolly flair,
While curious plants start to pair.

A parrot with a silly hat,
Dances tango with a fat cat,
While mangoes roll and try to groove,
In the shade, they find their move.

Cocktails spill from coconuts tall,
As the jungle hosts its grand ball,
Swaying palms, they shimmy and sway,
While the sun zooms off to play.

Mirth shines through the vibrant green,
As everyone joins the happy scene,
In this party of blissful fun,
Underneath the golden sun.

Tropical Symphony

In the land where colors burst,
Funky fruits bubble, ready to burst,
Bouncing to a happy tune,
As fireflies twinkle, night, and noon.

Lychee strums on a giant leaf,
Passion fruit sings, stealing grief,
Citrus notes blend in the air,
As coconuts roll without a care.

Lively rhythms fill the breeze,
As mangoes swing from jungle trees,
Each chirp and buzz joins the score,
Laughter echoes, who could ask for more?

Under stars, the fruits unite,
Crafting joy throughout the night,
With every pluck and every beat,
The tropical symphony feels so sweet.

Sweet Chords of Summer

In a land where sweetness plays,
Fruits join in a quirky craze,
Under sunbeams bright and bold,
Stories in their colors told.

Pineapples flash with a cheeky grin,
While cherries giggle, let the fun begin,
A coconut juggles with delight,
In this party of fruity light.

Mangoes sway in funky pants,
As grapes spin on dainty prance,
Watermelons bounce with sheer delight,
As summer tunes fill the night.

All united in fruity cheer,
Happiness spreads, far and near,
In every chord, the sun shines bright,
Celebrating each juicy bite.

Symphony of the Sweetest Fruit

In the orchard, laughter swirls,
A fruity dance, where joy unfurls.
The critters sing in silly tune,
As oranges jest with a cheeky prune.

Bananas swing from branch to branch,
While melons waltz in a merry dance.
The berries gossip, sharing glee,
About a sly lime climbing a tree.

Coconuts roll with a joyful thud,
Making friends with the playful mud.
Peaches chuckle, ripe and bright,
As cherries wink in golden light.

Each fruit sings in harmony,
Sharing love, pure comedy.
In this grove, nature plays,
A zany tune that never frays.

Echoes of the Orchard's Heart

Beneath the sun, the laughter spreads,
As apples tease the sleepy beds.
A lemon slips, and then it grins,
While kiwi joins in, full of spins.

Peaches prank with fuzzy tricks,
As plums do cartwheels, quick as flicks.
Pineapples boast of their fine crowns,
While berry brawls break all the bounds.

Tomatoes giggle, red as can be,
Doing limbo like it's carefree.
The grapes get tangled, snicker and sway,
In this orchard where games hold sway.

The fruits unite in joyful cheer,
Echoes of laughter, drawing near.
A sweet, silly symphony so true,
In this garden, where fruit's askew.

Tasting the Warmth of Paradise

From the tree, joy tumbles down,
As fig and date share a playful crown.
Mangoes plot with a wink and grin,
While papayas giggle; let the fun begin!

Citrus squirt in a friendly spray,
As cherries challenge to a juicy fray.
Bananas slip, but with a smile,
Their silly stunts are worth the while.

Watermelons roll with glee galore,
Singing songs that we can't ignore.
The fruit flies dance in wild delight,
As coconuts juggle, oh what a sight!

Paradise wraps us in its warmth,
With fruity pranks, it's a festive charm.
Life's too short to be so blue,
Join the laughter, there's fun to do!

Vibrant Notes of Nature's Lyric

In gardens bright, a concert's planned,
Where grapes strum strings with a gentle hand.
Lemons laugh with a zesty tune,
And all join in, from sun to moon.

The nuts play drums, a thumping show,
While avocados sway, stealing the glow.
Raspberries hum with a sweet, high note,
As they ride waves on a leafy boat.

Fruits are jesters, vibrant and bold,
With stories shared, and secrets told.
A lullaby of color, taste, and cheer,
In this melody, all hearts draw near.

Nature strums its funny strings,
Bringing joy with each note that sings.
In every fruit, a laugh is found,
Together we play, in joy unbound.

Dances in the Shade

Beneath the leaves, a party grows,
Where fruit in secret giggles and glows.
The branches sway as breezes tease,
And laughter bounces through the trees.

The squirrels join with acrobatic flair,
While birds pluck tunes from thin, sweet air.
All fruits unite in a jolly jig,
As bees buzz by, oh so big!

They twirl and spin in a sunny spree,
Each juicy friend as happy as can be.
With each plop and thud, they share their cheer,
The laughter echoes, loud and clear!

And when it rains, they dance anew,
Splashing puddles with vibrant hue.
So if you see them, don't delay,
Join the fun—come out to play!

Lush Melodies

In the orchard, a chorus sings,
With melodies only summer brings.
The fruits have found their inner voice,
In every plop, they rejoice.

Guava's laugh, oh what a sound,
While bananas sway, spinning round.
Pineapples nod, with hats so grand,
As oranges dance, all hand in hand.

A mango swings, it slips on cues,
With pulpy guts and sticky shoes.
They harmonize with juicy cheer,
While monkeys cheer and grab a beer!

With every note, the sun beams bright,
As fruits unite in sheer delight.
They twiddle and giggle, oh what a spree,
In the land where melodies roam free!

The Art of Ripeness

A canvas ripe with colors bold,
Each hue a story waiting to be told.
Green dreams shifting to a mellow gold,
As laughter ripens, the joy unfolds.

Nature's brush begins to play,
In the sun's warm embrace, come what may.
Each fruit a masterpiece, hanging fine,
With jokes so ripe, they sparkle and shine.

With every twist, a giggle springs,
As laughter sprouts from juicy flings.
In the gallery of senseless fun,
The fruits all shout, "We've just begun!"

The art of ripeness is no small feat,
With juicy punchlines—oh, what a treat!
So grab a brush, let's paint the day,
With giggles and joy, come out and play!

Nectar of Dreams

In a world where sweetness takes its flight,
Nectar drips, like stars at night.
Every sip a giggle meets,
Tickling tongues with fruity feats.

The bees collect the laughter fine,
Making honeysuckle dance divine.
With each drop, joy fills the air,
A nectar story that we all share.

Beneath the sun, they smile and drip,
Watch fruits tumble, and do a flip!
With zesty jokes, each tumbler beams,
In this land of sugary dreams.

So raise your cups to nature's play,
With laughter drizzled all the way.
In every drop, a funny scheme,
Join the nectar of our dream!

Sun-Warmed Soundtrack

Under sunlit skies so bright,
Laughter skips from left to right.
Juicy fruits make quite a scene,
Funny tales from trees so green.

A squirrel dashes, full of cheer,
Catching snacks, oh dear, oh dear!
While birds compete with silly tunes,
Dancing 'round like little loons.

Nectarous Verses

In gardens rich with colors bold,
Each bloom whispers, stories told.
Honeybees hum their sweet refrain,
Tickling petals, driving us sane.

A butterfly joins the parade,
With polka dots, a grand charade.
They twirl in joy, without a care,
Nature's jesters, up in the air.

Bathed in Sunshine

Sunshine drips like melted gold,
A heatwave of pranks, bright and bold.
Children chase shadows in a race,
While birds drop snacks with perfect grace.

Giggles float on the warm breeze,
As friends climb trees with joyful ease.
Each branch creaks under their weight,
Nature's swing set is first-rate!

Whims of the Wind

Whispers of wind, a mischievous chat,
Twirling leaves like a playful cat.
Rolling fruits across the ground,
A merry chase, lost and found.

Clouds drift by, wearing a grin,
As shadows leap, let the games begin!
Folks share jokes in the sun's light,
While laughter sparks, taking flight.

Whispers of the Breeze

In the orchard where laughter grows,
The fruits wear smiles, nobody knows.
A breeze tickles leaves, they giggle and sway,
While squirrels dance on branches, come out and play.

A plump little fruit rolled down with a thud,
Pleased to be messy—oh what a crud!
It laughed with the wind as it tumbled along,
Chanting a tune, a jolly old song.

The sun poked its face through the leaves so green,
Whispering secrets, if only they'd glean.
A butterfly flitted, teasing the air,
While ants tapped their feet without a care.

All around the laughter swirled and twirled,
Nature's own circus, a splendid world.
So join in the fun, don't miss the show,
In the orchard where giggles and whispers flow.

The Harmony of Sunlight

Under the sun where the giggles are bright,
Fruits pose for selfies, what a silly sight!
Bananas are laughing, proud of their spot,
While peaches flaunt fuzz that can't be forgot.

A pineapple wore shades, looked oh so cool,
Doing a dance, breaking all the rules.
"Let's party!" it shouted, "who's got the groove?"
Melons rolled in, busting smooth moves.

The berries formed bands, jamming all day,
With grapes strumming tunes in their funny way.
Under the warmth, they swayed and spun,
Making the laughter just bursting with fun.

So join this ruckus, don't stand on the side,
Dance with the fruits, take the fun for a ride.
In sunlight's embrace, let your worries melt,
With fruitastic joy that's truly heartfelt.

Orchard Overture

In the orchard where dreams take flight,
Fruits wear silly hats, a colorful sight.
A peach told a joke, a juicy old pun,
While the apples all cackled, oh such fun!

A coconut chimed in with a loud thwack,
Spinning in circles, it couldn't hold back.
"Who's ready for tumbling?" the orange did shout,
And all of the lemons laughed till they sprout.

Underneath branches, the giggles took flight,
As cherries had tea, what a wonderful sight!
With insects as orchestra, buzzing along,
They played such a tune, five-fruits strong.

So come to the orchard, where jokes are the key,
To a life full of laughter and pure glee.
Join in the overture, let your worries fly,
Under nature's circus, just laugh and sigh.

Melodic Juiciness

In the garden where taste buds sing,
Fruits chat and giggle, oh what a fling!
A kiwi wore glasses, looking so wise,
Sipping its juice, to no one's surprise.

Tomatoes threw parties, how juicy and red,
While cucumbers joked, making all laugh instead.
They danced on the vines, with rhythm so sly,
A splendid crescendo, oh my oh my!

Watermelon cannonballs in the sun,
Splashing sweet laughter, oh what fun!
With every big burst, a giggle is born,
In juicy adventures from dusk until dawn.

So savor the laughter, the sweetness, the joy,
In this melodic garden, come play like a boy.
Where flavors and chuckles delightfully blend,
In this scrumptious symphony, fun has no end.

www.ingramcontent.com/pod-product-compliance
Lightning Source LLC
Chambersburg PA
CBHW070005300426
43661CB00141B/244